Joys for the Journey

Inspirational Thoughts for RVers and Travelers

Joys *for the* Journey

Inspirational Thoughts for RVers and Travelers

Geraldine Wieland

New Leaf Press

First printing: February 1996

ISBN: 0-89221-321-3
Library of Congress Catalog No. 95-73133

Cover art by Dick Hafer

Unless noted otherwise, Bible Scripture is from the King James Version.

To my husband Walt, a cowboy from Horse Creek.
When the Road of Life threw him a horseshoe curve,
he maneuvered it with consistent courage and faith.

*The following pages contain short devotions for
a month's worth of vacation days, with several
extras thrown in, in case a snowstorm leaves
you stranded in a motel room, or your spouse
insists on making a wide detour to visit the
"World's Largest Ball of String."*

Happy Traveling!

THE FLEE MARKET
(Confessions of a Traveling Christian Writer)

"Readytogo?" came my mate's one-word query.

As president of his fan club, I tried to be flexible
When surprised by this spur-of-the-moment summons.
And though I seldom had my writing house in order,
I prayerfully packed the in-progress manuscripts and
Notified the post office to hold all checks and rejects.

Which of biblical Sarah's commitments were cut short
When Abraham "went out, not knowing where he went?"*
And maybe Mrs. Moses had just purchased a year's supply
Of papyrus for Hazeroth's Creative Writing Course
When the Pillar of the Lord signaled, "Readytogo!"

As pilgrims, Christians sometimes trade
Security blankets for things like portable typewriters;
In fact, the Lord commands, "Go ye," as long as there is
The message to communicate to those who might suddenly
Be called from this life before they are "readytogo."

*(Heb. 11:8)

Mile Marker 1

"Shouldn't we wait till you stop building houses before we start traveling?" I asked my husband.

My query was in response to his comment on the common sense of an ad in a local paper: *Will trade for pickup or trailer house of equal value, two cemetery plots.*

He'd read too many stories about folks who had *waited* to fulfill a dream, then lost their health, for example, and were left staring at an expensive, low-mileage motor home parked in the driveway, displaying a "For Sale by Owner" sign.

So, we took the credit cards and charged out, traveling in tandem for more than 101,000 miles of the United States, plus Baja and Canada.

And in the end, my husband was right. For after only a few retirement years, the Lord took him home.

Dear God, Thank You that we lose something in the translation — not only our aches and pains, but also our old sin nature.

And Enoch walked with God, and he was not; for God took him (Gen. 5:24).

Mile Marker 2

Perhaps the most difficult part of prolonged traveling is the preparation. Everyone from the paper person to the public utilities must be notified. Sometimes I felt like the cuckoo in the clock whose pre-midnight activity leaves only enough energy for three announcements during the subsequent two hours.

The pressure is on to pack the bags, but sorting your belongings leads to a desire to get rid of excess baggage. Setting your house in order, so to speak. I'd noticed that clean items moved faster at a yard sale. The trouble is the reason you want to get rid of things is that you don't want to work at cleaning them. Once renovated, they plead to be put back on the shelf.

Spiritually speaking, I suppose some folks shun salvation because they think they must go to the work of cleaning up their lives for God, and it seems like too much of a job. They don't realize it is neither possible nor necessary. In fact, it's a waste of precious time.

Dear God, As we plan for our journey let us also plan for opportunities to share the message that Your salvation is not a knick-knack to be polished and replaced.

The blood of Jesus Christ, God's Son, cleanses from all sin (1 John 1:7).

Mile Marker 3

Standing on the precipice of retirement is a New Year's Eve experience. Poised on one leg like a gorgeous egret, scanning the horizon for signs of assurance, one has a new respect for the Israelites and their step of faith into the Promised Land.

After many years of homework, it is indeed wonderful when God rings the recess bell. You are off to discover famous playgrounds which you have only read about. But don't wait too long or the National Park ranger will shock you by politely asking if you qualify for a "Golden Age" pass. And down the road a piece, you will discover that God was preparing you for another white-haired thought. Your sister's grandkids decide you must be their "great" aunt and uncle. Suddenly you recall the church social where the eight-year-old youngster said he was planning to run for president someday and he would appreciate your vote, if you're still living then.

Dear God, Football games appropriately kick off the new year. As we view the calendar squares (some already dotted with dental appointments, etc.) and evaluate our goals, help us to use our vital time-outs to recover from reversals and interceptions.

I have been young, and now am old; yet have I not seen the righteous forsaken, nor his seed begging bread (Ps. 37:25).

Mile Marker 4

How could we know our 6 grown children would take our 12 grandchildren and scatter like the little birds taking a "dust bath" in our unpaved driveway? (Bird-watching had set the pussycat's pendulum in motion, and evidently Mama Bird warned, "Cat approaching. Everybody out of the pool.")

So naturally, now that we had more discretionary time, we volunteered to go grandkid-sit when obligations called the parents away during the school year. And so it happened that while driving my granddaughters to church in their family car, the engine stalled.

The older one said, "Grammy, my dad had this car serviced just before you came, so whatever's wrong with it must be *your* fault." (Which made sense to me. In fact, it could be the story of my life.)

Dear God, I've always tried to color my pictures and drive my car within the lines. Isn't that good enough?

For by grace are ye saved through faith; and that not of yourselves, it is the gift of God — not of works, lest any man should boast (Eph. 2:8-9).

Mile Marker 5

Our nurse-daughter told about a 300-pound patient who asked her to hold his watch while he stepped onto the telltale scales. Obviously, he needed all the help he could get.

For me, cross-country motoring meant a "wash-and-wear" hairdo, the kind I could spritz with water and fluff into place. Anticipating this daily ritual, I'd filled an empty, non-aerosol hairspray bottle and printed WATER on it to distinguish it from the real hairspray.

One morning, when I was more awake than usual, the word WATER jumped out at me (just like an enlightening Scripture verse). Why, I suddenly wondered, was I carrying around a bottle of water? I could get water *anywhere*. (In fact, most states had more water than our home-base of drought-prone California.) I'd added eight ounces of unnecessary weight to an already bulging suitcase.

Dear God, I know there are no trivial sins, but if I deal with them daily, You can keep them from growing into cumbersome besetting sins — the kind that make me spiritually obese and disqualify me in the marathon of life.

Lay aside every weight, and the sin which doth so easily beset us, and let us run with patience the race that is set before us (Heb. 12:1).

Mile Marker 6

When visiting adult offspring, you will almost certainly get involved in one or two projects. The fellow who lived in the house our son was buying offered to help de-shingle the roof. At noon, I was dispatched with a coupon for take-out chicken and given orders to include cole slaw.

Since the "roofers" were tarred, if not feathered, we assembled outdoors for a picnic-style meal. The current owner went in search of paper plates and returned with his wife's grandmother's Spode china. I felt I should protest its use under such primitive circumstances, but he very casually responded that this was all they had. He was not impressed with their probable preciousness, being interested only in their present usefulness.

Dear God, Wherever we go today, may we sanctify You with our lips and our actions, never bringing shame to Your name.

Then they brought the golden vessels that were taken out of the temple of the house of God, which was at Jerusalem; and they drank wine, and praised the gods of gold, and of silver, of bronze, of iron, of wood, and of stone (Dan. 5:3-4).

Mile Marker 7

Roadside signs posted at the entrance to graveled, runaway-truck ramps amuse me the way they warn: NO STOPPING AT ANY TIME.

Obviously this admonition is not aimed at trucks with no brakes. But apparently other vehicles must be told not to block this area. It would be disastrous for a teamster to obey the NO STOPPING sign at the entrance to a sandtrap designed especially for slowing down his loaded tanker. On the other hand, an automobile driver *disobeys* it at great risk.

STOP ▬ ▬ ▬ ▬ ▬ ▬ ▬ ▬ ▬ ▬ ▬

Dear God, Your Word says that all biblical instruction is profitable. But some passages are more pertinent at certain times and in certain situations. Those with an education can read signs. Those with wisdom can read signs correctly. Like Elisha, I daily need double portions of Your discernment.

All scripture is given by inspiration of God, and is profitable for doctrine, for reproof, for correction, for instruction in righteousness, that the man of God may be perfect, thoroughly furnished unto all good works (2 Tim. 3:16-17).

Mile Marker 8

Springtime in the Rockies is photographing Colorado's white-faced cattle and black-faced sheep grazing on shirt-pocket pastures. But wintertime is a different story. Motorists must heed closure signs on roads in the higher elevations where engineers have done the impossible by subduing granite Goliaths. For just as man stands back to admire his handiwork, God sends a little snow and makes the impossible impassible.

We may try blasting our way through the difficulties of life, only to have God intervene for a season. Such roadblocks can be very disappointing. We want something to happen *RIGHT NOW!* So, we take our mental snowplow and push God's frozen flakes of circumstance off to the side of the road. (Psychiatrists call this "denial.") *Aha,* we think, *what's so hard about this?* Then another blizzard wipes out our progress. Experienced travelers obey all ROAD CLOSED signs.

Dear God, Today I once again discovered that my contrived snow-removal equipment is less effective than a toy truck. Help me remember that when You are ready, You will send the thaw I need to take me over the mountaintop of my troubles.

Lead me in thy truth, and teach me; for thou art the God of my salvation; on thee do I wait all the day (Ps. 25:5).

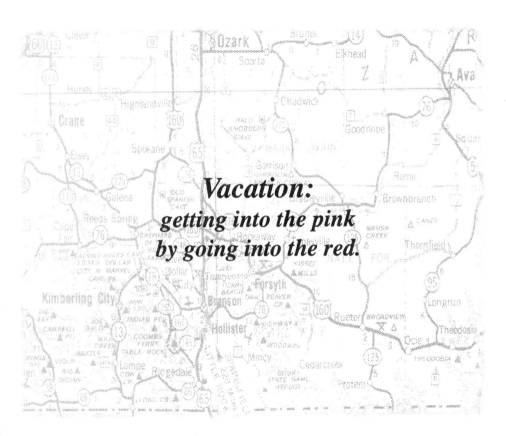

Vacation:
getting into the pink
by going into the red.

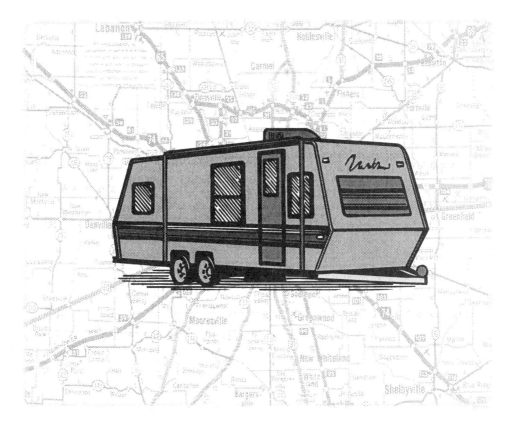

Mile Marker 9

Motel row blinked its neon billboards on the south side of town, and all-night freight trains trundled past, their whistles blaring like out-of-tune trombones. We'd found these accommodations only after our car had crept through a one-lane detour, adjacent to a lengthy stretch of construction.

All the way from the initial bond issue to the landscaping crews, building highways is an extensive and expensive job. Bulldozers rearrange real estate a little at a time, uprooting trees and dislodging boulders. Then other heavy machinery crunches along, tamping the freshly-graded trail. Continual maintenance will include either streuselling hot tar into cracks in marred blacktop, or unbuckling belts of uneven cement.

While Jesus prepares custom-built homes in heaven, He constantly oversees Operation Renewal on Earth. Heavy-duty Power is available for the hard-hat duty of prayer to pave the way for those who spread the gospel. Then the follow-up team takes over to provide ongoing care.

> **Dear God, May occupation with Christ motivate spiritual roadbuilding in Your earthbound occupation force.**

> *And he called his ten servants, and delivered them ten pounds, and said unto them, Occupy till I come*
> (Luke 19:13).

Mile Marker 10

Following our New Year's break-in, we proceeded to "lock the house after the jewelry was gone." In other words, we tightened our security and put some remaining valuables in a safe-deposit box. Still, I felt uneasy about leaving town, even for a few days. Would the interrupted intruder return for more loot?

At this point, the Lord reminded me of Ephesians 6:13. We had done what we could to protect our property. Now I needed to leave the matter in the hands of the Lord. Our shelter and our belongings are generous gifts from God. Not only is He Jehovah-nissi, He is also Jehovah-jireh, the provider of all our needs.

Dear God, If I forget today, please remind me that worry is a wretched traveling companion. It is emotional cholesterol incarnate.

Wherefore, take unto you the whole armor of God, that ye may be able to withstand in the evil day, and having done all, to stand (Eph. 6:13).

Mile Marker 11

Was it possible we were being escorted from this hospitable western state? What other reason would a patrol car have for trailing us on such a remote road? Finally, it went around us, and we fell into its 55-mile-an-hour pace, afraid to pass.

Sometimes the driver slowed to 50, seemingly distracted by an animated conversation with his passenger. After several miles of trying not to tailgate, our mini-caravan came to an underpass. Stuck in its craw was a truck with an oversize load and insufficient clearance, blocking both lanes of traffic.

When an orange-vested fellow emerged from "our" official vehicle, we realized this was a rescue mission (albeit, not a speedy one). Frustration turned to thankfulness for the presence of someone who knew how to solve the problem.

Dear God, Thank You that Your 9-1-1 number never has a busy signal. Before creation, You gave rescue Your top priority. Budget cuts cannot tamper with Your salvation for Your people.

Be not afraid of their faces; for I am
with thee to deliver thee, saith the Lord
(Jer. 1:8).

Mile Marker 12

Today we flew on eagle's wings in a 757. It took us up above the clouds, so close to heaven, and reminded us of You, our dearest friend, and the heights to which You go to lend a hand.

Someone is said to have counted the "fear nots" in Scripture and discovered one for every day of the year.

Childhood memories include summer nights of traveling into outer space by way of Dad's telescope. Focusing on the infinite was a delicate process. No one could touch the instrument while trying to peek at a planet. My favorite was Mars; that is until I read that it is encircled by two, tiny satellites, Phobos (fear) and Deimos (panic). If Mars is surrounded by fear and panic, then it is not my eternal destination.

Dear God, You keep reminding me to talk to You about my fears, and I keep promising to do it — later. Meanwhile, one normally functioning area of my life is out of commission.

And the angel said unto them, Fear not; for behold, I bring you good tidings of great joy which shall be to all people (Luke 2:10).

Mile Marker 13

Wyoming's Tetons looked like they'd been generously iced with countless cans of vanilla frosting. Midwesterners serve considerably larger hot cakes than those we grill at home on a California range. And just when I thought I'd solved the pancake caper by ordering only one, it turned out to be platter-size!

As swatches of yellow paint defined our descent, we wondered if the big breakfast was meant to be our last meal. Truck drivers were cautioned to stop for a brake-check before committing to this downgrade. The forest hid the canyon bottom, tinging the drive with apprehension. A blowout could send a vehicle over the edge.

"But the trees would cushion the fall," hubby reassured.

I'd read a news item about a seven-year-old girl who fell from a third-story, locked apartment. She was trying to escape because her mother had hanged herself. The youngster owed her life to a man who was walking by and caught her, thus cushioning her fall.

Dear God, Because I belong to You, whether a fall is accidental, or the result of desperation, I can know that underneath are Your everlasting arms.

Trust ye in the Lord forever; for in the Lord God is everlasting strength (Isa. 26:4).

Mile Marker 14

I liked their philosophy, "Our cook gets a day off. How about yours?" (One bonus of travel for the cook of the house is the joy of eating someone else's cooking.)

The restaurant hostess offered me a hot pink, wild rose from her garden. She'd enjoyed it all day and wanted to share. She said it was the first bloom from a bush which started as a barren, lifeless-looking stick.

The waitress explained that the mix-up in our orders was the fault of those in the kitchen — something I can't do at home. It's kind of neat to be able to blame others when things go wrong. Adam and Eve thought so.

Dear God, While almost any casualty calls for more than one culprit, You define responsibility as being in a position of having no one to blame but oneself. As I review my day, help me come to that place before You, realizing You are not going to let me implicate the kitchen help.

Behold, the rod of Aaron for the house of Levi was budded, and brought forth buds, and bloomed blossoms, and yielded almonds (Num. 17:8).

Mile Marker 15

When God gave us a mobile ministry, I typed and photocopied this leaflet, with a drawing of a license plate on the front fold:

Picking personalized license plates is fun, isn't it? We selected the restaurant term TWO TO GO when we missed out on our first choice of REDI 2 GO. But we won't miss out on being ready-to-go to heaven someday. A personal relationship with the Lord Jesus Christ assures that.

WHERE 2 was our third option requested by the DMV. We want to see all the scenery we can, while we can, but we are also looking forward to arriving at our Divine Destination. And we want you TOO TO GO!

Dear God, You can use the most insignificant things to turn a person to You. I pray you would use this tiny, hand-typed calling card to cause someone to call upon Your name.

And if I go and prepare a place for you, I will come again, and receive you unto myself; that where I am, there you may be also (John 14:3).

Mile Marker 16

At one observation overlook, erosion had done its Michelangelo work by sculpting huge red rocks into mammoth mushrooms. We exchanged photo-taking sessions with a farmer and his family. I gave him our gospel "calling card," which he accepted rather unenthusiastically.

Moments later we came upon an accident involving a half-dozen vehicles. Paramedics, modern-day Samaritans, were just arriving, and we realized, once again, that but for the grace of God we could have been part of a far-from-home pile-up. Once again an unscheduled sightseeing stop was part of God's schedule for us.

Dear God, recreational travel does not remove us from the realities of life. But even though accidents are not the kind of sights we set out to see, perhaps You allow us to pass by, so we can be silent Samaritans, praying for these unfortunate strangers who have been robbed of many things, including their peace of mind.

So if you consider me a partner, welcome him as you would welcome me. If he has done anything wrong or owes you anything, charge it to me (Philem. 1:17-18;NIV).

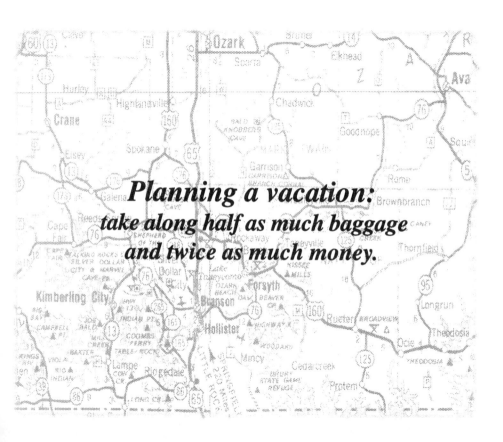

Planning a vacation:
take along half as much baggage
and twice as much money.

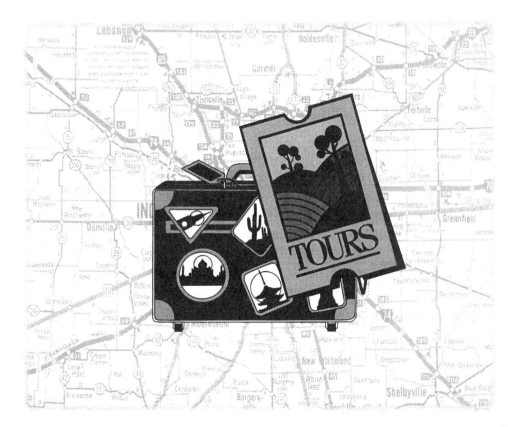

Mile Marker 17

The couple camping next to us in the RV park didn't like togetherness. So this morning I tried some friendly flattery, such as, "My, what a cute hat you have." The disgruntled lady said it was to cover the new perm she hadn't yet smoothed with the curling iron and asked if this was our first time here. When I nodded, she informed me the new manager should never have put anyone in our spot and warned that the park could expect to lose their business if they continued this policy.

"After all," she complained, "people come here to get away from it all, and they have a right not to feel crowded."

When we parted, she said to let them know if we needed anything, and I felt like I'd had my first lesson in everything you wanted to know about camping but were afraid to ask.

Dear God, When frustrations, like time-lapse blossoms, burst in bunches, I gather and clutch them in sullen impotence, denying any fragrance. But then, if I bring them to You, like a little child's offering to a parent, You reach for Your best vase and arrange them into an altar bouquet.

*Humble yourselves, therefore, under
the mighty hand of God, that he may
exalt you in due time* (1 Pet. 5:6).

Mile Marker 18

The family car is such that after miles of wear the brake or fan or clutch will surely need repair. But it never, ever talks to tell us where it hurts; instead, it simply balks or squeaks or squawks or squirts.

My least favorite job is that of apprentice when my husband assumes the role of auto repairman. Today I learned that when you are asked to lie down under a motorhome where a hydraulic jack is hovering over your head, it pays to listen to the still, small "ad-voice" inside of that head. I was certainly glad I'd shifted to the south because this one turned into a "jumping jack." My chagrined mate seemed to have no idea such a thing could happen.

In the end, he went to a garage where he'd made friends by returning a flashlight left in our vehicle after a previous mechanical operation. (Shouldn't truck "stops" be called truck "starts"?)

Dear God, The Golden Rule becomes more valuable all the time. And unlike gold, it never depreciates as a standard for human relationships.

And as ye would that men should do to you, do ye also to them (Luke 6:31).

Mile Marker 19

In pre-cruise-control days, we'd look for a bellwether car to follow — one going the speed limit — so we didn't have to keep such an eagle-eye on the speedometer. The trouble was that instead of finding such a car, we generally became one. Our steady pace brought us our own following.

It is not an accident that some citizens have better driving records than others. Obeying the speed laws can have other fringe benefits. For example, there is the blessing of not arriving until *after* a storm has "rained" its destruction. Similarly, obeying God means not racing ahead of His enabling grace. Also, after electing to put Jesus "in the driver's seat" of a life situation, it's time to tear up that coveted backseat driver's license.

Dear God, How many followers in life find out that they're unintentional leaders? If others are following me, let me log more miles in maturity by memorizing Your map — the Word of God!

But grow in grace and in the knowledge of our Lord and Saviour Jesus Christ (2 Pet. 3:18).

Mile Marker 20

With the temperature at 23 degrees and the wind-chill factor at zero, we watch the TV weatherman use his pointer-baton to direct the jet streams. With a flourish, he pulls a band of tropical moisture out of the south until it collides with a ridge of high pressure in a tympany of thunderstorms. Slowly he sways to the west where the symbols of sunshine strike their clear counterpart. Suddenly his fingers flutter in the snowy strains from the northern states. Winter must make weather impressarios very happy.

We had thought to go farther north today, but now we must decide whether to wait a day or two for a warming trend or scout out a more southerly route. Storms can be the barometer for the open and closed doors of recreational highway travel.

Dear God, It's in moments of great revelation when the course is so clear and the defensive smog-alert which dulled my perspective is gone, that I most need rescuing from the arrogance of thinking the future is a menu from which I'll always choose the most appropriate entree.

When they came to the border of Mysia, they tried to enter Bithynia, but the Spirit of Jesus would not allow them to (Acts 16:7;NIV).

Mile Marker 21

The pastor of the wayside church asked the congregation, "How many of you loaded your trailer last week and started out like Abraham, not knowing where you were going?" (I just about held up my hand.)

A road can cross town or pave its way across the country, but it probably won't get much wider than six or eight lanes. Still, whether I'm on an errand or an excursion, if I'm list-less or map-less my trip is aimless.

But God's call to Abraham to, "Go west, young man," could not be termed, "gullible's" travels. There was no need for Rand McNally; God was the camel driver. Did He direct the entourage along well-traveled trade routes, from oasis to oasis? Or did Abraham's faith-journey depart from the beaten track in the same way as his Exodus descendants?

Dear God, When I forget to thank You for journey's mercies, remind me how soon after the Red Sea rhapsody, the Union of Retired Bricklayers began singing the blues and giving Your rightful glory to a golden calf.

They have been quick to turn away from what I commanded them and have made themselves an idol cast in the shape of a calf (Exod. 32:8;NIV).

Mile Marker 22

The law-enforcement car races up the freeway ramp on its way to issue a citation. A motorist has failed to heed the warning, "Speed checked by aircraft."

From His heavenly viewpoint, God monitors the rate of His royal family's journey to joyful and holy living. Along the Christian way there are slow travelers and fast ones.

Even though we can't see God, He still sees us. It's as if the sky is a huge one-way window — the kind through which interns view a surgical procedure, or witnesses identify suspects in a lineup. While some portray God as peering down on humanity in a clinical or accusing fashion, most see Him as a loving Father expectantly looking for the return of His prodigal people and creating the heavens to shield them from the glory which would distract them from their duties here in the anteroom of eternity.

Dear God, My spiritual progress can be compared to the plants landscaping the freeways. Some areas flourish while others fail, having been assaulted by a swerving sedan. Today I confess that I've been sideswiped by Satan's traffic in anxiety.

And he arose, and came to his father. But yet when he was a great way off, his father saw him, and had compassion, and ran, and fell on his neck, and kissed him (Luke 16:20).

Mile Marker 23

Even today, waterproofing is an essential part of preparing an RV for the elements. Moses' parents faced an unthinkable decree which they no doubt prayed would either be changed or repealed. Casting the male Hebrew babies into the Nile wasn't exactly a popular command. But God showed them a creative way in which they could function within the framework of the law yet protect the child. The baby was placed into the river, but he was put into a prepared shelter first.

Dear God, When we wonder how You will turn a problem to our advantage and Your glory, help us remember that sometimes You will rescue from "within" rather than "out of" difficulties.

And when she could not longer hide him, she took for him an ark of bulrushes, and daubed it with slime and with pitch, and put the child therein; and she laid it in the flags by the river's brink (Exod. 2:3).

Mile Marker 24

We activated the air conditioner in the trailer and had the fans, TV, and typewriter whirring, blaring, and buzzing. Then suddenly our tiny electronic world shifted to a silent, sultry blackout. We blamed a blown fuse. (I thought of my dad's riddle, "Where was Moses when the lights went out?")

Subsequent flashlighted trouble-shooting revealed an extension cord almost "too hot to handle" — an obvious hazard. But since we belong to God, we decided this incidence was not a coincidence and that He must have sent some night-foraging critter to loosen the connection.

Dear God, all of nature is at Your disposal as messengers to care for Your people. Your light disperses our darkness.

Yea, the darkness hideth not from thee, but the night shineth as the day; the darkness and the light are both alike to thee (Ps. 139:12).

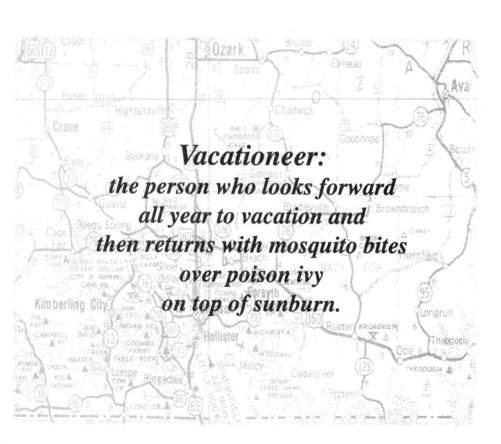

Vacationeer:
the person who looks forward
all year to vacation and
then returns with mosquito bites
over poison ivy
on top of sunburn.

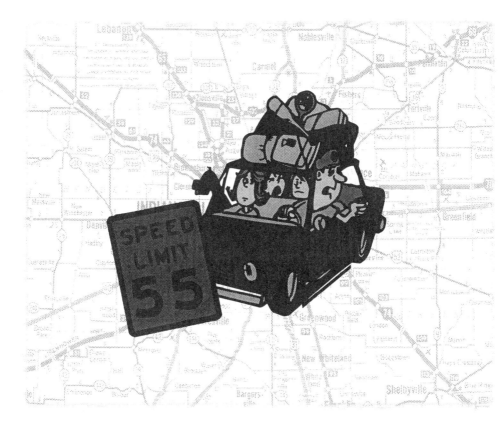

Mile Marker 25

The town was so friendly; it even had heart-shaped potholes.

The marquee bragged: Elderly menu/Native food. We couldn't resist.

We overheard a waitress giving travel directions to another customer. The lady wanted a shorter route to her destination but was told that the shorter way was not necessarily better.

I thought of Jesus standing at the intersection of the broad and narrow ways and pointing out where each will lead — yet giving each one a choice. The broad way is a dead-end street, while the narrow way is the thruway to God. Since the resurrection, Christ has posted believers at the crossroads to warn life-travelers that the only way to heaven is by way of the Cross.

Dear God, I wonder if cafes really mean to advertise, "Come as you are." Our "at home" eating habits would shock Miss Manners into a "first-person" viewpoint. The only tipping we do is to knock over a glass (full, of course).

On the other hand, Your invitation to "Come as you are" is infinitely and blessedly true. You wouldn't have it any other way.

Jesus saith unto him, I am the way, the truth, and the life; no man cometh unto the Father, but by me" (John 14:6).

Mile Marker 26

Travel calls for a certain amount of loitering in laundromats. We had this particular one to ourselves, and my waiting assignment was to transfer our past and present routes to a new, expensive atlas (the nomad's *other* bible). The yellow highlight streaks started flashing impressively, especially in the West and Midwest. Even Lewis and Clark would have been envious.

But alas, when we at last piled the suitcase-folded apparel into the auto, we forgot the atlas. Just a half-block away we realized our oversight and quickly U-turned. Again, no other customer or attendant was around, but neither was the atlas. Our old, taped-up map is a constant reminder of life's transient treasures.

Dear God, We are hard on ourselves when we are not perfect in the petty, inconsequential things of life, like burning the toast or taking the wrong freeway exit. But we make excuses when we are not perfect toward You. Truly, Satan would send us on a trivial pursuit of happiness by convincing us that overcoming our carelessness is the road to joy.

Lay not up for yourselves treasures upon earth, where moth and rust doth corrupt, and where thieves break through and steal (Matt. 6:19).

Mile Marker 27

When the freeway met the mountain, we saw the words most dreaded by motorists: LANE ENDS. MERGE LEFT. Signs and arrows warned of the return to two lanes.

Suddenly, double yellow lines hemmed us in, making us an insignificant segment of a serpentine of slow-moving semis crawling up the hill. We pushed radio buttons, seeking entertainment.

Oh, but how the words, PASSING LANE ONE MILE AHEAD, changed our attitude! Patience and hope became the "pass" words. No more "sweating it out."

Later, I thought about how the arrows of the Bible point to the invisible God. David's friend Jonathan signalled a warning by shooting arrows in a prearranged place. The plan was God's provision for David's protection, just as the highway arrows were for our safety. Arrows of warning have one target, as opposed to arrows of war which demand deflection. (Only if one has more war arrows than his enemy do they spell protection.)

Dear God, help me remember that Christians have the hope of a bright future.

Jonathan said to David, "Go in peace,
for we have sworn friendship with
each other in the name of the Lord"
(1 Sam. 20:42;NIV).

Mile Marker 28

When I left for church on Mother's Day, I supposed I would be teased for returning from four weeks of travel just in time to get my corsage for having the most children. In the end I was the one who got fooled, for after the roll call for the youngest and oldest mothers, there were no flowers left for fertility.

Even though spring had already spread her banquet of desert wildflowers, it was evident that love was still in bloom. The cement irrigation standpipes along our road carried spraypainted messages. The graffiti proclaimed the love of Elaine for another. Some of the pipes had hearts to emphasize her ardor.

Lovers no longer carve their initials into a tree trunk. That was a lot of work. And so permanent! Nowadays, Romeo courts Juliet (or vice versa) with an aerosol can. The final item concerning Elaine carried the admonition, "Trust me."

Dear God, How You love us and want us to trust You. As I travel through this time of my life with my "Roam-eo," there are signs everywhere of Your creative care for us. Every day is Valentine's Day as far as You are concerned!

Commit thy way unto the Lord; trust also in him, and he shall bring it to pass (Ps. 37:5).

Mile Marker 29

Raising our family in a rural setting meant either catalog shopping or a drive to the big city, with its well-stocked department stores. Even though the road eventually became monotonous, we still looked forward to our all-day jaunts because they included a binge at a gourmet buffet.

Even in recreational travel, tedious stretches of road can become bearable when the prize is seeing loved ones. Approaching the final, 40-mile marker our cheers go up.

"Just like going to the big city," we shout in unison.

Christians have a heavenly destination. Each day we draw nearer to our arrival at the Holy City. As we grow older we feel the excitement of all the rest and fellowship awaiting us. Even discouraged travelers can find new hope in a glimpse of glory.

Dear God, Thank You for life's temporary goals. They remind us of the reality of a permanent, yet unseen City. When we see signs we are getting close, please increase our sense of joy and anticipation.

And there was great joy in that city
(Acts 8:8).

Mile Marker 30

It was my turn to drive the first of several getaway vehicles we eventually would use, and I wanted to watch this odometer age its first one hundred thousand. So I began the countdown at 99,969 by singing this scriptural lullaby to my dozing copilot, "Seek ye first the kingdom of God," interspersing it with:

> Watch the speedometer turn all nines
> In only thirty-one miles,
> Then I will see all the zeros coming up
> A - lei - lu - lei - lu - ya.

Dear God, This seemed an appropriate serenade of thanks to You for all those safe, enjoyable miles of road-bounding, plus family bonding.

But seek ye first the kingdom of God, and his righteousness, and all these things shall be added unto you
(Matt. 6:33).

Mile Marker 31

Driving along, towing our fishing boat behind us, we saw a license plate with the challenging logo, "GO 4 IT." It voiced our goal of reaching our destination before dark because of temperamental trailer-light connections.

Getting a late start stirred apprehension. Would we make it? But, as the Lord would have it, we "sailed" into town just as the clouds, with their frosted, swept-back hairdos, framed the sunset's pink cheeks, and the sun seemed to be saying, "Hurry up and get home so I can set."

Dear God, You created mankind with a built-in longing for home. From this haven we hurry to send acknowledgments and promised photos to those who hosted us along the way, before "business as usual" gobbles up our good intentions.

But, first of all, may we remember that home is wherever we have the security of Your presence. In that sense, we never left home.

And, lo, I am with you always, even unto the end of the age. Amen (Matt. 28:20).

Mile Marker 32

While reading during less scenic, non-chauffeuring breaks, I grabbed a handy, refunded, parking-garage dollar bill for a bookmark. When I finished the book, however, I failed to return dear "George Washington" to my purse. Later, as we backed from a second parking space, we saw a fellow pick up a bill near the curb. And so it was that another rule of the road came into being: choose no $10's or $20's for bookmarks.

Monetary protocol followed us everywhere. Grandchildren brought out the silver dollars they'd squirreled away from our previous visits. Not only did they want to show Grandpa how thrifty they were, they also wished to remind him of his current donation. When he'd pretend he'd forgotten the tradition, they impressed him with tales of how they'd resisted the temptation to spend the hoarded coins at the local toy or candy shop. (Moms often confessed to being the banker for those with less frugal genes.)

Dear God, I was raised on the adage that "Money doesn't grow on trees," and I've found that true in my lifetime. But Your love, when planted early, can flourish on any family tree.

Either what woman, having ten pieces of silver, if she lose one piece, doth not light a lamp and sweep the house, and seek diligently till she find it?
(Luke 15:8).

July:
the month when mothers
realize why schoolteachers
need long summer vacations.

Mile Marker 33

One joy of spending the holidays with our oldest son and his wife was playing "king and queen for a day" while paying our respects to the prince of their domain.

As the couple prepared for an outing with friends, they hugged and reasssured their toddler about this alien called Grandma. (She'd brought gifts, and she'd said, "Ho, ho, ho," but she obviously wasn't Mrs. Santa Claus.)

I asked for phone numbers to reach them in case of emergency, and my son said he would wear his beeper "for my peace of mind." My pre-bedtime efforts to entertain the little one were continually interrupted by his disappearance into his room. When I eavesdropped at the doorway, I heard him dialing his play phone. It seems he was trying to reach his dad's beeper to request that his parents come home *right now!*

Dear God, There's nothing quite so ingratiating as having your wrinkle-free portrait done by a two year old wielding a purple, felt-tip pen.

Peace I leave with you, my peace I give unto you; not as the world giveth, give I unto you. Let not your heart be troubled, neither let it be afraid (John 14:27).

Mile Marker 34

Christmas light-seeing through an Austin, Texas, neighborhood brought exclamations of delight from the grandsons.

At one particularly spectacular front yard nativity and rooftop display, the younger one called from his window seat in the van, "Dad, stop! We should knock on their door and 'complicate' them!"

Aware of his embarrassment at our laughter, his dad remarked, "I think you mean 'compliment.' "

"Oh yeah," the little one said, with a grin.

Dear God: Hardly anyone expected Your Son to come to earth so quietly, as a baby, instead of as a king (although no one could hush the angels).

And now, hardly anyone expects Christ to return to earth with a shout, as a king, instead of as a baby.

Yes, many may not be expecting Your Son, but Your Scriptures say the angels will direct the crescendo of His coming again.

For unto you is born this day in the city of David a Savior, who is Christ the Lord (Luke 2:11).

Mile Marker 35

We'd had a tailwind rather than the predicted headwind for our flight down the freeway and arrived in town early in the afternoon. Our son's house was for sale. (Now we all know that a real estate person is someone who takes you out to see the "sites.") So when the agent happened to show up, we supposed she would let his weary parents into his house.

"I've heard *that* story before," she accused.

Apparently people claiming to be relatives had gained entrance to other residences for undesirable reasons. Suddenly we could picture pseudo-parents spotting a house on the market and staking it out in hopes some salesperson would "just happen" along.

Since we'd failed to stock up on doughnuts and coffee for our legitimate surveillance, we chose to dine at a nearby restaurant where I jokingly remarked, "Said one baked potato to the other potato, 'Foiled again.' "

Dear God, Some keyholes remind me of the one on the "lock box" to heaven. It is in the shape of a Cross.

I am the door; by me if any man enter in, he shall be saved, and shall go in and out, and find pasture (John 10:9).

Mile Marker 36

Sisters can react in opposite ways to a crisis. For example, when their family pickup was pulling the boat to a remote vacation lake, the truck developed mechanical troubles serious enough to require towing for repairs.

The older one began to fret and ask, "What are we going to do now?"

Once safely home from their outing, Daddy quizzed the girls on what they liked best about their trip: the swimming, the fishing, the hiking, etc. That's when the younger one admitted she thought the "most fun" was riding in a fancy-looking tow truck, equipped with a whining, electric winch and whirling lights which seemed to say, "Get out of my way!"

Dear God, Letting prayer be the first "think" I do in the morning will write the script for my acting and reacting during the day.

And the boys grew: and Esau was a skillful hunter, a man of the field; and Jacob was a quiet man, dwelling in tents (Gen. 25:27).

Mile Marker 37

It looked as if God had shaken a giant fig tree. The colorful fallout drifted overhead in search of the sunrise, and motorists parked both on and off the roadway. Would a professional photographer judge the sheet-metal sky a lifeless background for these iridescent teardrops? Once in a while a flash of flame appearing at the base of a balloon boosted it heavenward, taking these members of a floating congregation into a celestial sanctuary.

While I followed the airborne butterflies, a picturesque parable of pride came to mind. These beauties were filled with hot air. Back on earth they would once again be deflated blobs.

If pride is a problem, there is nothing more humbling than having a bike squirt in front of your car on a busy street. The tap on the knee the doctor gave you to test your reaction was nothing compared to the blow to the stomach you felt when your reactions were put to the test.

Dear God, Daily traffic incidents and near-misses call for the constant sacrifice of praise for that mysterious, God-given motor impulse called reflex action.

Pride goeth before destruction, and an haughty spirit before a fall
(Prov. 16:18).

East/west travel calls for the "shifting hands of time." Whose wristwatch should show the current time and which needs to be synchronized with the clocks back home?

Prearranged, long-distance check-in times will minimize the chances of talking to a beep. The term "answering machine" has to be a misnomer, for this electronic receptionist has no answers, only questions. Who are you, and what do you want?

My generation incurred no guilt-trips when projecting vocal chords across state lines. We waited for weekends or holidays and set the timer for three minutes. When it buzzed, we immediately replaced the receiver — goodbye or not. And whoever frivolously called Uncle Louie on his birthday got a scolding for not sending a card instead.

Dear God, When the bell dings on our life-span timer, and You remove us from this earthly oven of trials, we won't need to call Home. Eternity also means no need for a TICK TOCK DOC, as one clock repairman advertised. And since there will be no night there, we won't care that we can't collect on all that daylight we saved each summer.

And there shall be no night there; and they need no lamp, neither light of the sun; for the Lord God giveth them light, and they shall reign forever and ever (Rev. 22:5).

YIELD

Mile Marker 39

THIS IS A TEST . . . THIS IS ONLY A TEST! Around the country, radios periodically broadcast this message and follow it with an ear-splitting screech which is supposed to reassure the listener that disaster systems function properly.

I think they're called, "church hoppers." They're the folks who bounce from parish to parish with the attitude that, "This is a test." Lacking a specific standard for how much hospitality should be shown in order to pass their test, they simply measure each encounter with a subjective slide rule. I confess I've been known to return from a trip with a sad tale of being slighted by staid worshipers in St. Louis or Saginaw.

In His post-resurrection appearance on the Emmaus road, Jesus refused to be offended by His downcast companions. Instead, He went on to explain Scriptures pertinent to His fulfillment of prophecy. As a result, He got invited to supper.

Dear God, If I have my "snub-meter" vibrating on high-frequency, I will miss Your still, small voice speaking through spiritually, soul-piercing sermons. Indeed, true worship will fill me with the presence of Jesus, even in the midst of strangers. And I might even be asked to stay for the potluck.

For all the law is fulfilled in one word, even in this: Thou shalt love thy neighbor as thyself (Gal. 5:14).

Mile Marker 40

His family came to visit his grandparents, and it wasn't long before he discovered part of a mince pie. Now this was not a freshly-baked, homemade pie; it was the rejected portion of a frozen, home-baked one. To him, however, it fell into the very desirable category of dessert. But his requests always came at a moment which his mom considered inappropriate. Finally, his patience came to an end.

He opened the refrigerator and announced clearly through the frigid air, "I'm tired of not having any of that pie."

And as often happens in families, this phrase became part of the communal vocabulary. At first we repeated it in jest. We were tired of not having some tempting bauble. We were tired of hearing austerity bells clanging in our bank account. We were tired of having to postpone a trip because of yet another giant jump in gasoline prices. It shouldn't have taken as long as it did, but we finally realized we were just like that grandson — we had opened the forbidden door to discontentment.

Dear God, Forgive us for the times we fail to see that every cloud on our horizon is preparing us for a piece of Your spectacular pie in the sky . . . with real whipped cream!

In my Father's house are many mansions; if it were not so, I would have told you. I go to prepare a place for you (John 14:2).

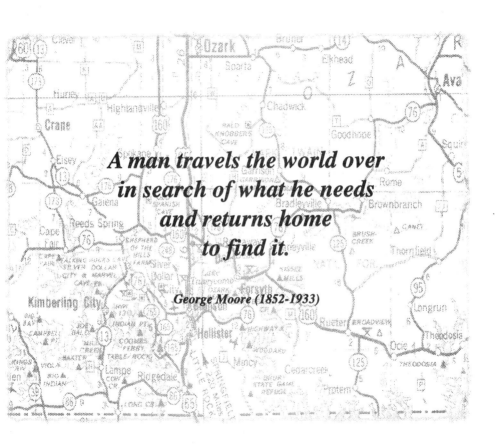

A man travels the world over
in search of what he needs
and returns home
to find it.

George Moore (1852-1933)

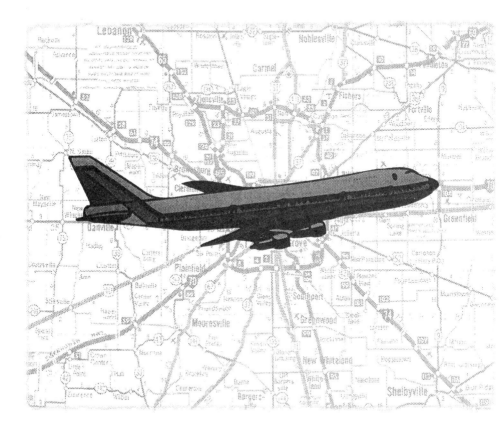

Mile Marker 41

"I'll wait in the car if you want to take a look at it," my weary husband volunteered.

Having missed the turnoff to Montezuma Castle National Monument, we were in the parking lot of Arizona's Montezuma Well. But after bouncing between bushes and through dry washes warning against entering when flooded, we still weren't *at* the well. It was hidden at the end of a walking trail behind a little hill.

This stop came near the end of a day's outing. We'd already rubbernecked the beauty of Oak Creek Canyon and accomplished the heights of historical Jerome. As I elected to retreat to the freeway, I wondered how many of God's blessings I'd missed by stopping short of a goal. The Bible tells of a Samaritan woman who came to draw water from the town well. What if she also had turned back on that day when Jesus was there?

Dear God, Montezuma Well was described as being cup-shaped. A cup of water indicates a sacrificial, unselfish gift. Thank You that Your vital gifts of compassion and blessing are always available to the weary traveler seeking spiritual refreshment.

But whosoever drinketh of the water that I shall give him shall never thirst, but the water that I shall give him shall be in him a well of water springing up into everlasting life (John 4:14).

Mile Marker 42

One of the mixed blessings of travel is selecting suitable souvenirs for those who agreed to "stay by the stuff."

WINDOW SHOPPING
No half-priced bargain, this designer mug!
Kiln-dried, with curving lip and sturdy handle,
It beckoned from a sleek, boutique display
While my checkbook held its stingy breath.

Will embers of immense enjoyment
Spill warmly over the ceramic rim,
As she perceives my rare extravagance
In joyfully relinquishing restraint?

Dear God, "Salvation" looked expensive,
So I resisted asking for Your lavish Gift
Until there came that momentary choice —
Then ultimate God-life flowed into me.

They shall be abundantly satisfied with
the fatness of thy house, and thou shalt
make them drink of the river of thy
pleasures (Ps. 36:8).

Mile Marker 43

He knew his ATM/PIN number was 30-something; he just couldn't think of the other two digits. This temporary amnesia didn't deter him, however. He pressed on, impatiently trying various combinations — without success. Finally he had to get his cash inside from an animated rather than an automated teller.

Later that week, after several errands, he again needed funds. But his time he was armed with the correct secret code. *This* time there would be no trouble. But there was! Instead of twenties, he got instructions to contact a bank officer. Alas, it seems that his previous experimenting had caused the machine to block access entirely. This block, meant to trap thieves, could only be removed by someone who believed the cardholder's explanation and verified his identification. This fellow's failure to "bide his time" led to both frustration and embarrassment.

Dear God, Help me remember my prayerbook is not a checkbook — with many more urgent demands for payment than praise deposits.

But they that wait upon the Lord shall renew their strength; they shall mount up with wings like eagles; they shall run and not be weary; and they shall walk, and not faint (Isa. 40:31).

Mile Marker 44

Touring the nation's burgeoning breadbasket brought to mind a poem of contrast I'd written about a California couple:

AVERTING CROP FAILURE

Our neighbors bought a tiny, rural plot
And buried there some beneficial seeds:
Zucchini, but no zinnias in that spot,
Just edibles to meet their basic needs.
Those gardeners eschewed insecticides,
Electing to raise their food organically.
With purity and wholesomeness their guides,
They refused to harvest crops mechanically.
And when these farmers sought to share with us
The life-sustaining produce they had grown,
We welcomed it, for then we could discuss
The "Priceless Seed" God in *our hearts* had sown.

Dear God, You sent Your only Son down from above, so we could share Your everlasting life and love.

*But he that received seed in the good
ground is he that heareth the word,
and understandeth it, who also beareth
fruit, and bringeth forth, some an
hundredfold, some sixty, some thirty*
(Matt. 13:23).

Mile Marker 45

In recent years I've noticed a resurgence of the "Noah's ark" phenomenon. A customer can't buy just one mousetrap or eyebrow pencil. They are packaged in pairs. Perhaps it makes sense to have a pencil for each eyebrow, and maybe one should assume that an invading mouse has a mate.

Someone endeavored to build a better mousetrap by arming it with a pre-baited square of plastic Swiss cheese. This is what caught the rodent that climbed aboard our stored motorhome. But I'm sure that if a mouse stowed away on a spaceship, no astronaut would endure an encore of bruised fingers from trying to set a spring trap. (Were poisoned pellet packets manufactured to forestall this unlikely mishap?)

In our case, I was appalled when my spouse turned the crippled critter loose, assuring me of its inability to return. (But I noticed he reset the trap — just in case.) And sure enough, the next night we heard the telltale snap and found our undaunted mouse-burglar had climbed to its destruction.

> *Dear God, How we praise You that through the ages You've never resorted to the convenience of commercial, twin-packaging in designing Your perfect plan for each individual.*

> *And of every living thing of all flesh,*
> *two of every sort shalt thou bring into*
> *the ark, to keep them alive with thee;*
> *they shall be male and female*
> (Gen. 6:19).

Mile Marker 46

I understand that automobiles, like computers and elephants, now have memory. One can program a car seat for instant driving comfort. For someone who has always thought of a back pillow as standard equipment, it must be heaven!

When in the course of family events, it becomes necessary to borrow Mom's car, she never gets the same car in return. It may look like an identical vehicle, even to the scratch on the left-rear door, and may even have a full tank of gas, but it is not the same car. The driver's seat and the mirrors have been repositioned to someone's superior height, and there's no way for a mom, who's been brought up short, to reclaim the exact setting where her foot can reach the gas pedal without her knee touching the dashboard. It's a little like being the designated adjuster on a motel TV which, for anti-theft reasons, hangs from the ceiling.

Dear God, Did You put the story of Zacchaeus in Your Word just for me? How comforting for someone who feels physically looked-down-upon to know that Jesus looked up and noticed a tiny tax collector.

And, behold, there was a man, named Zacchaeus, who was the chief among the tax collectors; and he was rich. And he sought to see Jesus, who he was, and could not because of the crowd; for he was little of stature
(Luke 19:2-3).

Geraldine Wieland began her traveling days at 18 months when doctors advised her dad, a mustard gas victim of WWI, to go out West for his health. The family of three, along with the paternal grandparents, left Connecticut in an early model Ford, converted into a camper. The toddler said, "See cow," and "See horse," for 3,000 miles.

After her conversion to Christ in her mid-thirties, Geraldine taught Sunday school and Bible clubs. Twice-widowed, she is active in her church and writing group, and visits her six children. She is called "Grandma Gerry" by her 12 grandchildren and two great-grands and the pre-schoolers she reads to at the library. She has published poetry plus inspirational and humorous articles, including a lighthearted regional column for seniors titled "Gerri-Atrics." Geraldine lives in North Highlands, California. This is her first book.